RONAN
and other stories

David Thomson

M
MACMILLAN

Illustrated by Liz O'Sullivan

For Ivy

Copyright © David Thomson 1984

All rights reserved. No part of this
publication may be reproduced or
transmitted, in any form or by any means,
without permission.

First published 1984 by
MACMILLAN CHILDREN'S BOOKS
a division of Macmillan Publishers Limited
London and Basingstoke

Associated companies throughout the world

Filmset in Optima by Filmtype Services Limited,
Scarborough, North Yorkshire.

Printed in Hong Kong

Series Editor: Gail Barron

Designed by Sue Williams

ISBN 0 333 365771

Contents

Ronan	4
Jo-al-ticitl	19
Ahto	40
The Poison Damsel	53

Ronan

Long, long ago in the days when all the birds and animals knew how to speak, there lived in a village on the west coast of Ireland a young fisherman called Finn and his wife Cara.

Finn's hair was black. Cara's was red with glints of fire in it, like the tips of the rushes. They had a little baby boy just six months old whose name was Ronan and he was a fine strong baby and happy most times, but whenever the wind rose and the sky was black and the waves of the sea turned white and lashed the cliffs below their house, spattering their windows with spray, he would be crying night and day.

"What ails him?" said Finn one night when the sea was wicked.

And Cara said, "He is that way, restless, when the storm is on."

Finn looked down on him in the cradle and said, "He is not afraid."

And Cara said, "He is never afraid of the storm. It is more as if he would walk out in it if he was old enough to walk."

One day in September when the sea was calm Ronan's mother had to go to the fair to sell her eggs. There was no way from the village to the town where the fair was held except by sea and she and all the young people of the village climbed on to a large sailing boat to cross the bay. She put Ronan into Finn's arms and said, "Mind him well until I come home."

Finn went up the cliff path home with the baby, laid him down on a lock of hay in the potato garden and took up his spade to dig there, very near to him, watching him from the corner of one eye. He wasn't long digging till a neighbour leapt over the wall.

"God bless the work," said the neighbour whose

name was James.

"'Tis a grand day for it," said Finn.

"It is," said James. "And it is a grand day to go into the seal cave and catch a seal."

"I cannot go with you," said Finn. "For I must mind the baby. You must look for another man to go with you."

But all the other young men were away at the fair. James's sea-boots, which were made of sealskin, were quite worn through. He had no oil left for the lamp at home, and it was seal-oil that all the people used for their lamps in those times.

"It is a pity," he said to Finn. "For one big seal would make boots and waistcoats for every man that needs them, and meat and oil for all the people of the village. And I am afraid", he said, "lest this be the last calm day before the high seas of winter close the mouth of the seal cave to us."

"I cannot go with you," said Finn and if he said it twice he said it seven times. But James would not let him be.

"Well now," he said, "I'll tell you what we'll do. You will bring that little baby with you to the seal cave and lay him in the boat. He'll be just as well off in the boat, and the day sunny, as lying here in the potato garden."

"A very good thought. I'll take him," said Finn, but the raven walking on the short grass near the garden croaked three times.

The raven said, "Carry Ronan to his cradle."

But Finn wrapped Ronan in a blanket and they set off.

The seagull whirling in loops above their heads screamed, "Far away, far away! Can't you catch the cry of the storm?"

When they were halfway down the cliff, the grouse who was feeding on the heather at the top cried, "Go-back. Go-back. Go-back."

As they rowed along in the shadow of the highest cliff a mother otter looked out from her cave and whistled, "Fear this, fear this, fear this!"

And when they came near to the huge dark mouth of the seal cave the stormy petrel flitting past on the surface of the waves said, "See me! See the storm! See what I see!"

But neither Finn nor James paid attention to these creatures. They moored their boat outside the seal cave by fixing a spike of its anchor into a cleft in the rocks and waded into the darkness of the cave. Finn laid the baby on a dry flat ledge of rock just inside the mouth of the cave and the baby was even more happy than usual, talking to itself.

"Now that is strange," said Finn to James, "for every man that comes into the cave is afraid as you are now and as I am. But Ronan has no fear."

A little daylight from outside cast ghostly lights on the rippling water in the cave. On its black roof and over the dark ledges mysterious shadows flickered. The men were up to their waists in water.

"We had best go back," said Finn. "I can hear Ronan crying." And the echo of his voice came back to him — "Crying. Crying."

"That is not Ronan," said James, "That is a baby seal. There is no difference in the sound."

Then a voice no different from a woman's cried, "Finn! Finn!"

He caught James by the shoulder and stood still, much afraid.

"Don't kill me," cried the voice, "till I give the breast to my little one." And the echo said, "Little one! Little one!" all round the cave. Looking up to the ledge in terror, James saw a big mother seal with a pure white baby by her.

"I won't kill you," he said. "Nor ever again in my life will I kill a seal."

At that moment the cave became even darker than before, there was a shriek like a whirlwind, and a great wave came in and took the men off their feet. As it subsided they swam as fast as they could to the mouth of the cave where a bigger wave swamped them. They plunged through it and came up to the surface just beside their boat.

It was only when they were rowing away from the cliff where the waves were fiercely breaking, that they remembered the baby, Ronan. The sea had risen and covered the mouth of the seal-cave by then. Some of the waves swept up the cliff and broke at the top four hundred feet above. There was no way back into the cave.

Finn and James went sorrowfully home. Cara was there. Her boat had landed safely just before the storm began.

"Where is Ronan?" she said. "And where were you?"

When he told her, she wept with anger at him for what he had done and she wept for her lost baby for two days and two nights and all the people of the village came to the house to mourn the baby for two days and two nights.

On the morning of the third day, when the sea was calm enough, James and Finn went back into the seal-cave to look for Ronan's corpse. They saw nothing in the darkness except the mother seal lying with what they thought were two baby seals.

"Leave her alone," said Finn, and they went home.

One of the babies was Ronan.

All that time while his parents and their neighbours were grieving for him, he had been very happy. When the great waves that nearly drowned his father came roaring into the cave, splashed up to its roof and streamed down the rocky walls he was babbling and lalling with pleasure.

He watched the shining water and the moving foam, the drops that fell glistening in the half light from above and went "La-la. Da-da-da-la", and just as he was beginning to feel cold he felt a large warm body beside him. It was hairy. He put his face against it, just as he always did against his mother's breast, and found a teat like hers full of milk. Sucking beside him lay another baby, warm to touch and covered with soft white fur.

Within two or three weeks he had grown very fat and could crawl or at least pull himself along the ledge on his tummy. All his wrappings had fallen off by then because his seal mother kept rolling him about with her nose and flippers whenever she wanted to get him into the proper position for feeding.

Day after day she took him and her seal baby to the water, deeper and deeper day after day until they learned to swim and dive. Swimming under water was more difficult for Ronan than for his sister because she could close her ears and nostrils just as one closes one's mouth, but he soon learned to stay under for a long time, and at last they were able to swim out to the open sea. They swam and caught fish with hundreds of other young seals. Their mother left them.

Ten years went by and Finn and Cara had six other children. It was a happy family. But Cara said, "If Ronan was alive, there would be seven and seven is a blessed number," and every year, on the day of the September fair, she and Finn were quiet and went about their work thinking of Ronan and saying prayers for his soul.

On the tenth fair day after the loss of Ronan, James came hastening to the house, calling, "Finn, Finn!" He had spent his breath clambering fast up the cliff from the strand and could say no more, but the raven walking on the short grass croaked three times, "Ronan! Ronan! Ronan!" and Finn was afraid because the raven can see all things and this being Ronan's deathday, he believed it had seen Ronan's ghost.

"Come quickly," said James when his breath came to him, "There is a white seal lying there on the strand — a rare seal."

"I will never again kill a seal."

"I am not asking you to kill him, but to look at him before he slips back into the water. He has not one hair about his body but the hair of his head falls over his shoulders and is red."

"James, I misdoubt you," said Finn and he laughed.

The seagull whirling in loops above the house cried, "Catch the creature. Catch the creature," and Finn said to James, "Did you want to catch that seal?"

"I have a strong fishing-net on the strand, but it would take two men to close it over him."

"Well, James, I'll go with you if you promise before God to do no harm to that rare seal."

James gave his promise and they set off.

Halfway down the cliff, when the strand came into sight with the small waves breaking on it at low tide, Finn stopped. He counted twenty seals lying there below on the sand, all mottled grey and tawny yellow.

"This is a foolish business we are at," he said. "We'll go no further."

"The white one is smaller than the others," said James. "It lies hidden between two big ones," and the grouse, who was feeding on the heather at the top of the cliff, cried, "Go down! Go down! Go down!"

They went down, took the net and held it out between them like a curtain, crept up to the seals and stood between them and the sea. It was then that Finn saw the white seal. All the others veered away and plunged into the water but the men dodged in front of the white one and threw the net over it. It struggled and fought, tore the net with its teeth and wailed and moaned so pitifully that Finn said "Let it go!"

"No," said James. "We shall first show it to Cara. If she says 'Let it go', we shall carry it back to the sea."

They carried the white seal home in the net and put it down on the kitchen floor, and all the children came to look at it and said, "That's not a seal. It's got hair on its head the same colour as Mother's."

"Don't touch it," said James. "It will bite."

But the children pulled long strands of seaweed from its hair and untangled many beautiful seashells from the matted ends, and it did not bite.

When Cara came in she pushed the hair from its face and looked. "That's strange," she said to Finn. "It has a nose and eyes like yours!"

"It has lips and hair like yours," said Finn.

Then Cara cried out, "It is my son! It is Ronan!"

Ronan lived at home with his three land brothers and his three land sisters from that day on, but he never forgot his seal sister. He went swimming and playing with her every evening. And in winter when the great storms were on he would be in the sea or on the rocks day and night. He saw every fishing-boat that was in danger near the rocks, took its rope in his teeth and pulled it, swimming through the fearful waves, to the shelter of the quay. He dived deep after drowning fishermen and carried them safely ashore.

Soon he was the hero of the village. All the people of the village called him King.

Jo-al-ticitl

Jo-al-ticitl was named after the goddess of cradles, the goddess who had the biggest family in Mexico — millions and millions of babies in millions and millions of cradles and millions and millions of boys and girls who ran about and played. No one on earth could count them, but the goddess knew them all and all their earthly mothers, for she was the Great Mother of the Aztec people.

Little Jo-al-ticitl lived in a mountain hut with her mother and an ogre. There were only two rooms in the hut, a little room where the ogre slept on a pile of bearskins and a large room where she slept beside her mother on a crimson blanket on the floor by the fire. There was a wooden chest in one corner of the room, a thick oak table in the middle and one three-legged stool.

They had no other furniture but on the chest and on the table and on the floor by the walls stood jars and jugs and bowls and pitchers – round ones and thin ones and tall ones and fat ones and huge ones shaped like barrels. Jo-al-ticitl's mother had made all these out of clay, and baked them in the embers of a bonfire to harden them and turn them red, the colour of old bricks.

She had drawn magical pictures on the jars in black, white, blue and gold of gods and goddesses, animals and birds, and when they were empty, if you tapped them with a wooden spoon, they rang like bells and could be heard far, far away at the top of the highest mountain. They were Jo-al-ticitl's books which she loved and looked at every day.

Her favourite was the biggest pot of all. It was more than twice her height and even on tip-toes she could not reach its rim, but looking up she could see a picture that terrified her — a mother bear with three cubs running away from a hunter. One arrow was flying towards them through the air and the hunter was drawing his long bow to aim another.

On her birthday, when she became seven years old, her mother said: "Come. This is a special day. You will have your breakfast at the table. Sit on the stool."

Jo-al-ticitl shook her head and whispered: "It is his stool." She and her mother always ate their food squatting on the floor.

"Come," said her mother, "he is asleep."

Jo-al-ticitl sat on the stool and began to eat her breakfast which was a bowl of porridge made of Indian corn-meal, but she was only halfway through when they heard the ogre groaning in the room next door.

Her mother touched her elbow. She slid off the stool and ran to her dark corner where her three baby bears lay asleep. She picked them up and cuddled them and stroked their fur with her cheek. They were really three pieces of wood she had found in the forest, and their fur was the yellow brown moss that had grown on them.

Her mother brought her bowl and wooden spoon to her and ladled out the ogre's porridge from the big black cooking-pot which hung from a hook over the fire.

The ogre was so tall that he could not stand upright inside the hut. He stooped and shuffled towards the table with his arms hanging down and his thick hands dangling over his knees. No one could ever see his face because of a huge black beard that came up to his eyes and the long black hair that covered his shoulders and forehead.

Jo-al-ticitl's mother put his porridge on the table, but as soon as he sat down he stood up again because the stool was warm. He shouted: "You've been sitting on my stool, you good-for-nothing!" He threw the stool at her. "Why aren't you working, you lazy woman? The sun is up over the mountain and here you are indoors!"

She took her hoe and went out, holding her daughter by the hand. "If we could find some honey, it would sweeten him," she said, and she began to dance, and all the way to the plantation Jo-al-ticitl and her mother danced together in the early morning sun. And as her mother danced she sang:

> *The crimson colour of the God of Day*
> *Is reddening the mountain.*
> *He is reddening the Heavens*
> *As he sends the night away.*
> *Soon, soon he will put on golden garments*
> *And travel high*
> *Through the white and blue sky!*

And Jo-al-ticitl sang: "White and blue sky, sky!"

On her birthday, when she became twelve years old, her mother said: "Come. This is a special day. Put this on."

She held out a long red dress with blue and gold patterns on it, which she had woven out of goats' hair. Jo-al-ticitl had worn nothing but a loin-cloth until that day. She put the dress on. It came down to her ankles and its golden collar touched her chin when she looked down at her toes.

She was happy, but only for a moment because the ogre came out of his room in a rage and threw the stool at her. "Why aren't you working, you lazy girl?" She went for her spindle to spin more thread and he went out.

"If we could find some honey..." said her mother.

Jo-al-ticitl took off her dress because she knew she could not run in it, put an empty jar on her head and ran far into the forest till she came to a wild bees' nest in a hollow dead tree. She put her arm into it and touched the sticky honey but the bees stung her and she ran away. She ran with a cloud of bees over her head till she reached a pool of water and plunged in head over heels. There she stayed underwater, coming up for breath like an otter every now and then, until the bees went away.

As she was about to climb out of the pool, she heard a deep growl and a snuffling, gurgling, sloshing, slubbering sound. She turned and saw a big round furry face reflected in the water, yellowy brown, with black shining eyes, a black nose like a dog's and round golden ears standing up wide apart like little cups on end.

It was a huge bear drinking. Of all the bears she had seen in the forest there was none like him. He was larger than any of the others and on his forehead there was a black mark like a horse-shoe.

Jo-al-ticitl was cold and afraid, but she thought it safer to stay where she was with the water up to her neck. She stared at the bear and when he had finished drinking he stared at her, and said:

"What are you doing?"

"I am looking for honey."

"Honey? In the pool?"

"The bees stung me."

"Have you no fur?" he said. "Get out and let me see you."

He sounded so cross that she obeyed and stood trembling in front of him in her loincloth. Her skin was the colour of honey, dark honey such as bees make from heather. She told the bear about the ogre and how she had left her empty honey-jar beside the wild bees' nest.

"I shall fill the jar for you", said the bear, "if you will promise to meet me at this pool in five years time and to do whatever I ask you to do."

"What will you ask?"

He would not say. She gave her promise and led him to the hollow dead tree. She hid in a thicket where the bees could not reach her and watched him plunge his paw again and again into their nest. They could not sting through his thick fur. When he had filled the jar he took it in his teeth to her and she balanced it on her head and ran home.

On her birthday, when she became seventeen years old, her mother opened the wooden chest and took out of it a pair of silver earrings set with dangling moonstones. She said: "Come. This is a special day. Wear these," and she began to dance and sing a sad slow song:

I lie down with you, I rise up with you.

If my earrings tremble in my ears,

I know it is you moving in my heart.

"Why are you sad?" said Jo-al-ticitl.

"Because your father cannot see you with these earrings."

"Where is he?"

"In my heart. He died when you were one year old."

When the ogre walked through the hut in a worse rage than ever, Jo-al-ticitl said to her mother, "I'll go for honey," and she ran through the forest to the pool with an empty jar on her head. The bear was lying by the pool on his back, sunning himself and waving his huge paws aimlessly like a baby. He said nothing when she asked him to get honey for her. He just stretched out his arm and pulled her down by the waist on top of him, holding her against his furry tummy with her face touching his chin.

"Will you marry me?" he said.

Jo-al-ticitl burst out laughing. He held her tightly and said: "Have you forgotten your promise, five years ago?"

"To do whatever you ask me to do," said Jo-al-ticitl, remembering and trembling with fear. "Must I marry you, then?"

"Yes."

"Where shall we get married?"

"If we swim together in this pool we shall be

married."

They swam together in the pool.

He found a wild bees' nest and filled her jar. "Climb on my back," he said.

With her on his back and the jar between his jaws he ran up the mountain towards the ogre's hut, swinging, swerving, swaying in and out the trees, jumping from rock to rock, tossing her up and down. She felt sea-sick. She thought she would fall off. She called to him to go more slowly but he seemed not to hear. She gripped his fur with her toes and fingers and she dug her teeth into the big tuft on his neck and held on there as well.

When they came near the hut she told him to hide while she took the honey to her mother. Then she ran back to him and they went away together.

All that summer Jo-al-ticitl and the bear wandered up and down the slopes of the forest eating fruit and honey, searching for berries in the scrubland where the bushes were thick and for insects among the rocks lower down. She did not like eating insects. He used to turn over huge stones which she could not even lift and gobble up hundreds of creatures as they tried to run away. He was so greedy it made her laugh.

"I am five times bigger than you," he said, "and I eat nothing all winter."

When his tummy was full he would gaze about him, swinging his head from side to side with an absent-minded look and then lie down in the sun.

The sun was too hot for her because she had no fur, so she always lay beside him in the shade of his body but sometimes he rolled over on to his back and almost suffocated her. He was playful and she loved him.

But when the autumn came he had no time to play. He was eating all the time – walnuts and acorns, manzanilla fruit, nuts from the nut-pine tree, small animals which he dug from their nests in the ground, and sometimes corncobs and beans from the ogre's plantation. Jo-al-ticitl tried to stop him going there but he was stubborn and greedy. He grew very fat.

When the snow began to fall he said: "Come. We must go up into the high mountains."

"Why?" said Jo-al-ticitl. "The snow will be worse up there."

"We must go to sleep," he said.

They climbed the mountain for a day and a night and another day and a night in the snow until they came to a sheltered cave. The bear scraped the snow from the doorway and pulled a big bush up by the roots to make a door. Inside there was a springy bed made of branches and thick dead leaves. Jo-al-ticitl was delighted.

"It is cosy here," she said. "No fire. But you will keep me warm in your arms." She kissed him.

"You can't stay here," said the bear.

Jo-al-ticitl burst into tears.

"I shall find you a den not far away," said the bear. "And we shall meet again in the springtime when the weather begins to be warm."

And so she understood that all bears live alone in the winter and sleep for four or five months.

"But what shall I eat?"

"You won't want to eat."

"But I shall be lonely."

"You will have babies. You won't want me."

With his claws he dug a round den for her and dragged into it some leafy branches for her bed. She liked it but she cried and cried when he left her there.

She lay awake all night. The wind whined and shrieked. The wolves howled. And she was cold. She thought of her warm furry, loving bear and of the long winter alone. She shivered and her earrings trembled. She sang her mother's song for him:

> *I lie down with you, I rise up with you.*
> *If my earrings tremble in my ears,*
> *I know it is you moving in my heart.*

She could not sleep. At dawn she decided to go home to her mother but the snow had drifted ten feet deep against the mouth of the den. She lay down again. She prayed to her namesake, the goddess of cradles, to give her a baby before she died of starvation.

Her skin began to tingle. Her legs were itchy and when she scratched them they did not seem like her legs at all. They were covered with fur. Her tummy and her back began to tingle, her arms and neck and face felt itchy and when she scratched them one after another she felt fur. She touched the backs of her hands with her lips and they felt furry. She clasped her hands and found that her fingernails had grown into thick long claws. She had turned into a bear.

Now she did not feel hungry. She felt sleepy. She slept for two months, all day and all night, and then one day at noon when a little light was shining through the snow at the mouth of her den she woke up with a pain in her tummy and her first baby was born. The second came half an hour later and the third a few minutes after that.

They were blind like kittens but quite naked with no fur on them at all and all three of them together weighed less than one human baby. Jo-al-ticitl licked them all over with her long bear's tongue and went to sleep again while they sucked her milk.

When she woke up in the springtime they were as big as newborn lambs and covered with thick brown fur. They ran about the den and played together and with her. They were fat and she was terribly thin. Their tummies were full of milk and hers was empty.

Most of the snow had melted from the mouth of the cave and they all climbed out together and made their way down the mountain through the forest until they came to the verge of the ogre's plantation. They hid under the bushes and she looked through the leaves across the cornfield at the doorway of the ogre's hut. She was longing to show her children to her mother, but dared not move until she found out where the ogre was.

When a great big bear walked into the cornfield and began to nibble the young green shoots she tried to warn him to go away by growling. He was the thinnest bear she had ever seen. She growled again and when he answered her she knew his voice.

"Come into the bushes and hide," she said.

"The ogre is up in the high mountains. I saw him on my way down," her husband said.

So they all went together to the hut.

When Jo-al-tacitl's mother saw them she was very much afraid. She came out with her hoe in her hand to drive them away. Jo-al-ticitl tried to show her earrings but they were covered with fur. Then she stood on her hind legs hoping to be recognized, but that made her seem more terrifying than before.

Her mother ran back into the hut screaming, took up a long wooden spoon and tapped the biggest pot of all, the one with the picture of bears on it, and it rang like a bell and the wind took the sound far up into the mountains where the ogre heard it. Thinking that the house was on fire or that robbers had come he turned back. He could run and jump from rock to rock as fast as a mountain goat.

The bears did not hurry away. Jo-al-ticitl went on talking to her mother through the door, hoping and hoping to make herself known. Her husband wandered back to the cornfield. Her children clawed her legs to make her lie down and feed them.

37

Then suddenly she heard a fearful hissing like a snake flying through the air and saw her husband fall with an arrow quivering in his side. She saw the ogre standing at the corner of the field with his long bow. She ran to hide with her children behind the hut but — hiss, hiss, hiss — they fell beside her. She stood over them, licking them, but she knew they were dead. Then she felt a sharp pain in her heart and fell down over them.

Her mother watching from the doorway thought all five bears were dead. Then she saw a tall stranger walking in the cornfield and when she looked at the dead mother bear it stood up. Its fur went away, its face changed. It was Jo-al-ticitl, and beside her stood two little girls and a boy. She ran to them and hugged them, and then she said: "Look!" The stranger was approaching.

"It is a prince," she said. "What can I offer him in this poor hut?"

Jo-al-ticitl looked and saw a prince in golden garments and a jewelled crown. On his forehead beneath the crown, as he drew near, she saw a black mark like a horse-shoe. She took her children by their hands and ran to him. He was her bear, her husband.

"We were under a spell," he said. "We had to die before we could turn into people again."

The ogre was hiding, frightened by what he had done. But the prince found him and thanked him and said: "Come and live with us." And he built a palace out of marble and silver and gold and jade and onyx and starstones and moonstones and sunstones and he and Jo-al-ticitl and her children and her mother and the ogre lived happily in it for the rest of their long lives.

Ahto

Once long ago near the icy north of the world where in winter the day is as dark as the night and in summer the sun shines all night and all day, there lived a Prince alone with his old father, the King.

One morning in the month of May the King said, "Come to me, beloved son, and listen. Do you hear the soft breezes from the South as they nurse the young leaves and gently rock the branches? Do you hear the liquid song of the river which cherishes young fish, and the music of the birds who guard their eggs with care?"

"I hear them," said the Prince, "but I hear no calves this month of May, no foals nor little lambs that play."

"The Ice King killed their mothers," said his father. "All winter he stretched his icy fingers down the ten rivers of our country and took away their water. He spread his snowy beard upon the pastures and took away their food. Go now to the King of the South, whose land is warm and plentiful and ask him for a bull and seven cows, a ram and seven ewes, a stallion and seven mares. Tell him that his gift will be returned threefold in time."

The Prince mounted his swiftest horse and chose as his companions three skilful herdsmen whose horses were hardy and sure-footed, whose dogs were wise to the ways of cattle, sheep and horses.

In the evening they came to a mountain lake and when they and their dogs and horses had quenched their thirst, the Prince lay down to rest.

"Do not lie here, my lord," the herdsmen said, "for in this lake lives Ahto, God of the Waters, who drags sleeping men to the bottom." But the Prince said, "Ride on. Pitch our tent on dry ground and I shall follow you." They rode on.

Soon he heard a sweet sound of bells coming from behind a high black rock. He walked round the rock and saw five reindeer grazing with bells on their necks and a girl who was milking one of them, kneeling on one knee.

When she saw him she lost her balance and fell, spilling some of the milk. She had never seen a stranger before. He helped her up and saw her dark hair rippling like the river, her eyes quick and bright as the brown trout, her lips red as the rowan-berry, and he said, "Will you marry me?" She pushed him from her and went on milking.

When she had finished she gave him some milk in a wooden bowl. He drank half of it, then held the bowl to her lips. She took it in both hands and drank, looking over its rim into his eyes and although she said nothing he knew she was saying "Yes".

She led him up the mountain, and he led his horse, to a little round house made of earth and grass, with beautiful wild flowers growing on its roof, where she lived with her parents and younger sister. Her father was a holy man and in the morning he married them. The herdsmen came to the wedding and then rode on towards the South. "I shall stay here three days and three nights," the Prince told them, "and then I shall overtake you on my swift horse."

On the fourth day he gave his bride a precious ring, saying, "Go to my father's palace in nine months' time and show him this, and he will know we are married. In nine months' time I shall come to you there."

"Why so long?" she said, and wept.

"It is three months' journey to the Country of the South, riding fast, and six months' home with the animals."

Nine months later, she and her sister set out for the palace on a reindeer sledge but they were only halfway there when she stopped the sledge, took the rugs out and laid them on the snow telling her sister that she had a pain and would lie down. She lay down and her sister helped her and she gave birth to a baby boy.

A little later, after nursing the baby, the Princess felt sleepy. "Take care of the baby, dear sister," she said, "for I must sleep a while." Her sister laid the baby on the rug between them and watched it, but the long sledge journey had made her tired and soon she too fell asleep.

Now there came through the birch trees in the darkness another young mother, a wolf, who had had her cubs the night before near that place and carried them home one by one to her den. She had come to see whether she had left one behind and finding the baby she picked it up gently in her teeth by the back of its neck, just as she had picked up her own babies, and brought it home.

When they awoke, the Princess and her sister saw her tracks in the snow and followed them but soon lost them in the tracks of other animals. They searched all night and then travelled on to the palace in despair, and when the Prince arrived after his long journey expecting his wife to be as joyful as he was he found everybody dressed in black. They told him that the baby had been eaten by a wolf.

"I do not believe it," said the Prince.

As the Prince was saying those words, his baby was fast asleep in the wolf's den. Four baby wolves lay with him in a bundle clasping their front legs over him, keeping him warm against their mother's side. He was happy and full of wolf's milk, just as they were.

He was brought up with the wolf cubs in a dark cave beneath a high black rock beside a lake and when he grew big enough he went hunting with them at night. He ran on all fours and soon learned to keep up with the pack. Sometimes he swam across the lake with his wolf brothers and sisters.

For seven years the Prince and his huntsmen and herdsmen searched the pine forest and the birch forest, the rocky caves of the mountains, the thickets in the plains and the black caverns near the banks of the rivers. He and the Princess had one other child, a little girl called Brita, and every year in the month of May they took her to stay with her grandparents at their grassy house in the mountains, where they had first met.

One evening in the seventh summer Brita, who

had been playing by the lakeside, came running home in terror. Her grandfather who was sitting on a log at the entrance to his house, said, "Stop, my wild calf, and say what tore your heart to send you running up the hill as though a pack of wolves were at your heels."

"I saw Ahto, the water god."

"Was he black or light?"

"He was black in the lake when his long hair shone floating. He was light on the rocks when he came out and ran away."

"Did he run on two feet or four?"

"On four. And he had four dogs that climbed out of the water and ran away with him."

"Where did they run?"

"Through the thick rushes beneath the black rock."

The old man took his pestle and mortar that night, and ground up aniseed from the strong-smelling seeds of the wild plant anise, together with other aromatic herbs which attract dogs and wolves. He gave the mixture in a large leather pouch to the Prince and told him to lay a trail of the powder all the way from the black rock to the palace. He told the Princess to go home to the palace with Brita.

"Why must we go so soon?"

"A stranger will come there tonight. You must be there to welcome him."

"Who is it, father?"

"Someone you lost seven years ago."

The Prince laid a trail from the black rock to the palace steps and late that evening he hid inside the palace doorway. At midnight he saw five wolves running towards him, their noses to the ground. At the top of the steps, where the trail ended, they turned round and round not knowing where to go, but one which seemed braver than the rest walked into the palace sniffing about him.

The Prince closed the door and shut the others out. He knew that this strange wolf without a tail, with long black hair on his head and very little on his body, was his long-lost son. The Princess knew it too.

Brita came running and cried out, "That is Ahto!", much afraid.

"It is your brother," said the Princess, and they named him Ahto because he had come out of the water.

He would not let anyone touch him. They put a plate of food and a bowl of water on the floor and went to bed, but Brita did not sleep. She crept downstairs and peeped at her brother. His plate was empty and he was asleep, curled up on the floor with his knees against his face. Now that she knew he was her brother she was only a little bit afraid.

She went on tiptoes and sat beside him, and cautiously stroked his hair. Then she fell asleep. When her mother came down in the morning she saw them lying in a bundle. Ahto's arm was over Brita's neck, her head beneath his chin. Through the windows the Princess saw four big wolves sitting on the palace steps.

Only Brita knew why Ahto was unhappy. Only she understood the wolfish sounds he made, what he meant when he licked her face. She asked her father to open the door and let the big wolves in.

Everyone in the palace, except her father, her mother and the old King ran away to hide. The wolves came in warily nosing about till they found the scent of Ahto's hands and feet. Then they rushed to him and leapt up on him, bit his neck playfully and licked him all over. He ran with them round and round in circles.

They leapt into the royal drawing-room and tore the cushions, shaking the feathers up in the air and trying to catch them; into the banqueting-hall where they pulled down the tapestry and tore it to shreds; into the great kitchen where they gorged themselves on meat and fish till they were so full they could not move, but fell asleep under the table. Ahto slept with them. Brita who had run after them everywhere, laughing, lay down beside him.

Ahto's wolf brothers and sisters lived in the palace from that day on. They loved him even after he learned to speak and to run and walk upright. It was Brita who taught him. He copied her.

Ahto grew up, and when the time came to return the gift of animals threefold to the King of the South, he, along with his wolves as herd-dogs, took three bulls and twenty-one cows, three rams and twenty-one ewes and three stallions and twenty-one mares all the way across the mountains and through the warm Southern plains, and when the King of the South saw his strength and skill in herding he gave him half his kindgom.

Ahto married the daughter of the King of the South and they lived happily together with the wolves for the rest of their lives. But they often came home to the North to see his parents and they often brought Brita to the South to stay with them in their palace.

The Poison Damsel

The ancient land of Sizire was dry and hot. Its rocky mountains shone like copper in the sunlight and like silver under the moon. Its vast desert, which took a camel caravan thirty days to cross, sparkled with gold dust and tiny diamonds each the size of a grain of sand. But these riches meant nothing to the people or even to their King. Water was to all of them the most precious thing in the world.

The King had a daughter named Zahour. When she was twelve years old, wandering through the desert with her father and his people and their camels and horses and tents, she dreamed one night that she was walking in a dark cavern, deep underground, and she saw a great mirror lying there gleaming with light.

When she woke she led the people to the place she had dreamed of and told them to dig with their long poles. They bored seven times seven deep holes there till they reached an underground lake and seven times seven fountains of pure water sprang up. The animals and people who were dying of thirst drank blissfully.

Soon many green plants and shady trees grew there — the tamarind, the tamarisk, the fig, the pear, the persimmon and the pomegranate — and the people built many white flat-roofed houses and a temple with tall jewelled minarets and a royal palace, white, with a golden dome and silver cupolas on its roof. Here Princess Zahour lived with her father until he died and she became Queen of Sizire.

Soon after she became queen, she had an evil dream. She dreamed that the king of a distant country had invaded Sizire at the head of a thousand horsemen whose spears glittered more brightly than the gold and diamonds of the desert. They took all her people away as slaves and this strange king was binding her arms and legs with silken cords when she woke up.

She sent for her Soothsayer, the wisest man in the land, and told him her dream. He said, "Your dream is true. Last night a baby prince was born in a distant land. In three times seven years he will ride into Sizire at the head of a thousand horsemen and make you his slave. Last night a beautiful baby girl was born in this city. Her mother died in giving birth to her. Last night the Great Snake that lies outside your palace walls laid seven eggs. Place the baby girl inside the seventh egg and she will save your country and your people."

The Great Snake was poisonous. If a man smelt her breath or looked into her eyes he would fall down dead. When she stretched herself out her body twined all round the walls of the palace and she lay with her head at one side of the palace gates and the pointed end of her tail at the other. The people going in or out picked fig leaves and pressed them to their faces, lest they should see her eyes or breathe her breath.

Her body was thicker than the belly of an Arab mare and her eggs were as large as barrels. Only the Queen could look into her eyes and breathe in her breath, for the Queen had magical powers.

The Queen of Sizire stepped down the seven steps of her palace and took up the Great Snake's seventh egg and carried it into her chamber. She sent for the beautiful baby girl and placed her inside the egg. With the egg in her arms she stepped down the seven steps again and she gently placed the egg beside the other six where she had found it.

Time passed and six little snakes hatched out. From the seventh egg a little girl emerged. She had black hair and a long slim body.

At first, when the people saw her, they thought she had a tail instead of legs for she held her legs together and her arms close to her sides and wriggled over the ground with her brothers and sisters, playing with them, twining her body round them as they twined theirs round hers. She ate snakes' food as they did. She hissed when something frightened her as they hissed. She was poisonous as they were. And all the people pressed fig leaves to their faces as they watched her. The Queen named her Zahabah.

When the young snakes grew up and left their mother for the desert, the Queen brought Zahabah into the palace and kept her in a golden cage. She did not stand or sit in it. She slithered round its floor.

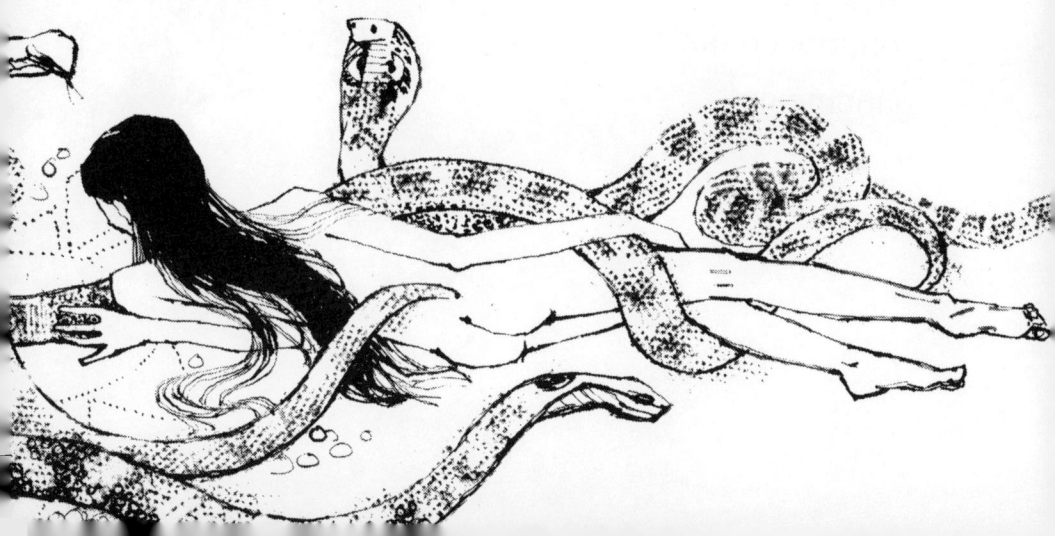

She could not speak. She only hissed. And when a courtier, attracted by her beauty, came too near he fell down dead. Soon she was known as the Poison Damsel.

On her seventh birthday, the Queen began to feed her with bread and gradually she taught her to speak and to stand upright.

On her fourteenth birthday the Queen clothed her, called for the royal harpist to teach her to play the harp and summoned the dancing girls to teach her to dance.

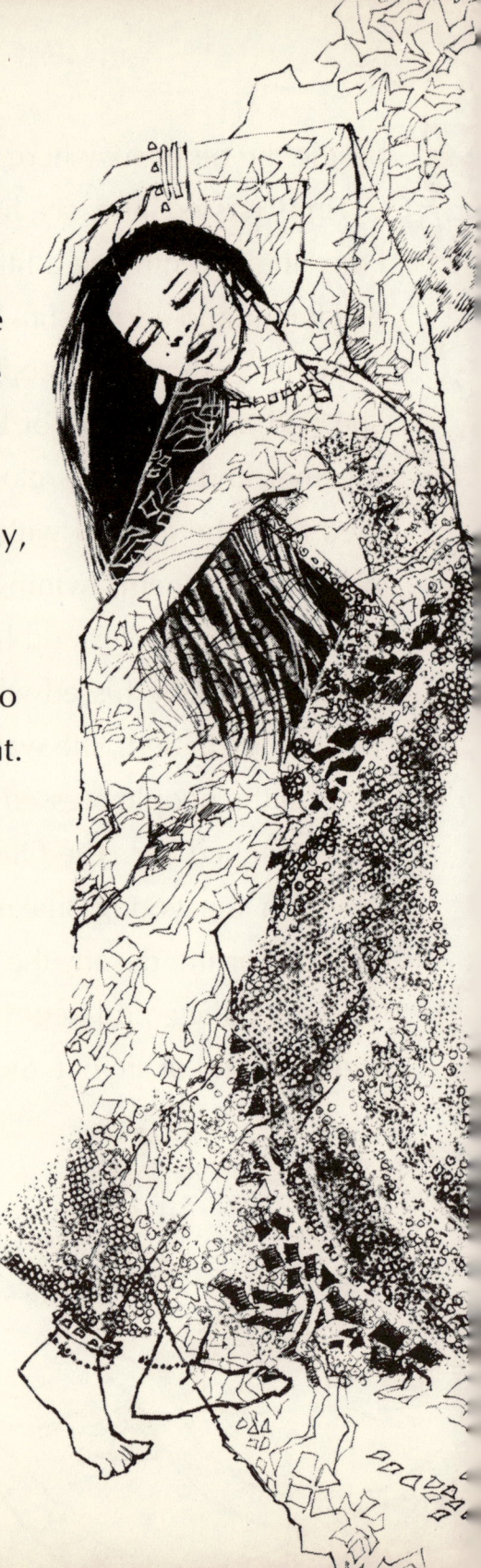

On her twenty-first birthday, the Queen dressed Zahabah in a splendid robe and adorned her with a necklace of moonstones, with sapphire earrings that dangled like tears beside her cheeks, with silver bracelets hung with golden bells, with golden anklets hung with silver bells.

For safety, the people stood far from her as she danced at her birthday feast, as her body swayed like a beautiful snake, as her arms and legs coiled and reached out like the children of a snake. When she played the harp and sang, they wept at the sadness of her music and the poetry of her song.

At the height of the feast a shining stranger came among them and word reached the Queen that a thousand horsemen, whose spears were glittering in the starlight, had gathered at the palace gates.

"Who is that damsel?" said the stranger to the Queen. "She that sings sadly like a goddess who is cast from heaven to the earth. She that dances lively as a snake, whose eyes are two limpid pools, whose ears are delicate as carved ivory, whose lips are round as the ripe, red cherry and on whose carnelian cheek I see a little mole which is a dark tear shed by a star which looked down from heaven and wept with black envy of her beauty."

"Go near to her," said Queen Zahour. "Look closely into her eyes, place your lips on hers and taste the sweetness of her breath."

Then the Queen sent all the people out of the great hall and left the stranger alone with Zahabah.

Zahabah put her harp aside and glanced at the stranger as he walked towards her. One glance was enough to make her fall in love with him and she quickly raised her arm to keep him away. He stood still. She lowered her eyes and gazed at her toes and said,

"I am Zahabah, the Poison Damsel. If you look into my eyes or touch my lips with yours you will die."

The stranger said, "I am the king of a distant country. I came into the Land of Sizire to take your Queen and all her people into slavery. But now that I see before me the most precious jewel of Sizire, I shall go home peacefully with my thousand horsemen, if I am allowed to bring you, the most precious jewel, with me as my queen."

Zahabah looked at her toes and said, "My snake mother shed her skin today. Only a belt made from her skin and clasped around my waist by your hands will take the poison from me. Only a breastplate cut out of my snake mother's skin and placed upon your breast will save you from my poison when you come near me with the belt. Take with you the oval mirror that is hanging on the wall and if my snake mother comes near you hold it before her face."

The Great Snake, at ease in her new skin, was resting in the pools beneath the fountains, her tail coiled in one pool, her body looped in another and her neck and head dipping in and out of the deepest pool of all which was opposite the gates of the palace. When she saw the stranger King come down the seven steps she raised her head and hissed.

He found the tail of her old skin lying near the palace gates. It was striped green and black. With the point of his sword he cut a belt from it just long enough to fit Zahabah's narrow waist. And he walked on round the walls of the palace till he reached the middle of the snakeskin where its patterns, gold and red, were shaped like the leaves of the lotus plant.

As he drew his sword again to cut a leaf-shaped breast-plate for himself, he heard a sound like a poisoned water-spout and saw behind him the long glistening length of the Great Snake sliding towards him, her head reared high, her forked tongue flicking.

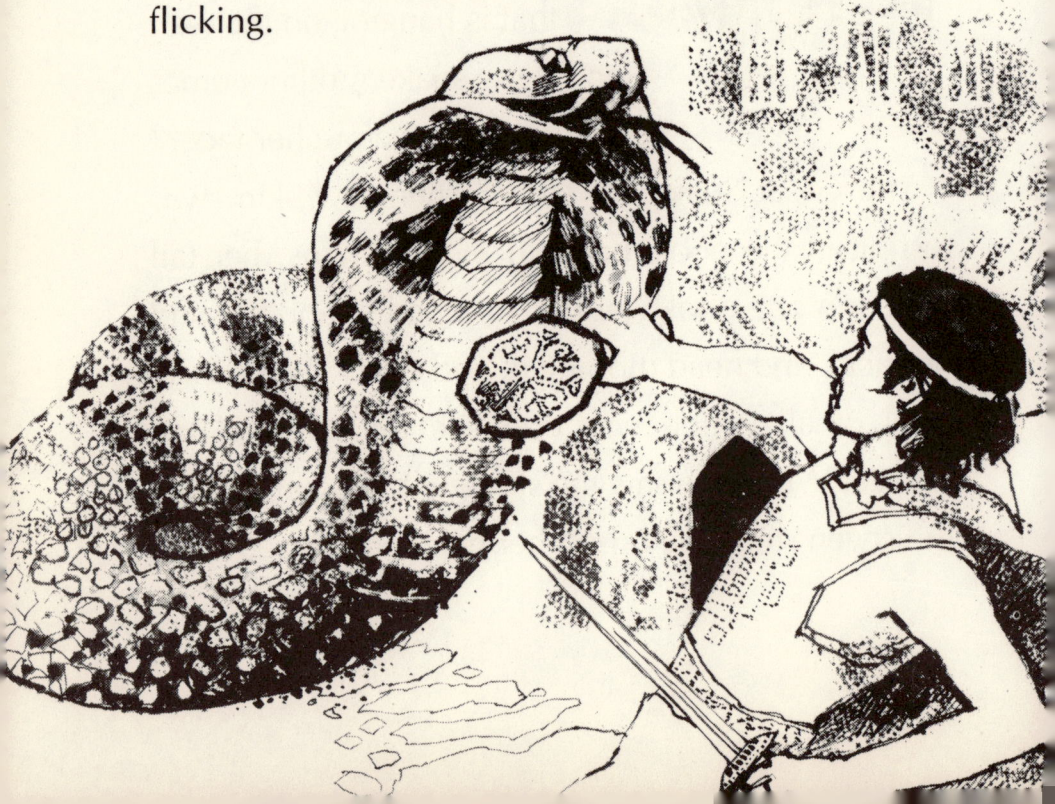

He was just in time to hold the mirror to her face. In it she thought she saw another snake and she kept still, fascinated by the fierce beauty of that strange snake. He cut out his breast-plate, put it on and returned to the great hall of the palace.

When he had clasped the snakeskin belt around Zahabah's supple snake-like waist, she allowed him to kiss her and they went hand in hand to the Queen's chamber.

When the Queen saw the stranger King alive and saw him press his cheek against the Poison Damsel's cheek she gasped with fear and fell in a faint at his feet. He raised her up.

"Give me Zahabah's hand in marriage," he said, "and she shall be my queen. And I shall depart peacefully from the Land of Sizire with my thousand horsemen and their thousand spears which gleam in the starlight and in the sunlight and cast a cloud of fear upon your people."

Zahabah's birthday feast was splendid. Her wedding feast was royal. She danced with a hundred dancing girls and then she danced her own snake dance alone. When she played the harp and sang the people wept with joy to hear her blissful music and afterwards came up to her to kiss her without fear for all the poison had been taken from her by the love of the stranger King.

And when the feast was over the Queen of Sizire presented Zahabah with nine white she-camels and nine white she-asses, each with a black cross upon its shoulders and a black stripe on its back, so that she would have asses' milk and camels' milk on her journey across the desert, and to the stranger King she gave nine black he-asses and nine dark camels, so that their herds might multiply, and to them both she gave ninety-nine of the swiftest pure black stallions, ninety-nine sorrel mares and ninety-nine mares of the purest cream.

Zahabah and her husband, the stranger King, embraced the Queen of Sizire and bade her farewell. They crossed the desert safely and reached the distant land where they lived in peace and plenty until they died of old age.